# God Has Not Forgotten YOU

# Now

# Is The Time

BY

## Beverly M. Jones

*All my Love,*
*Beverly*

Published by
INSTITUTE OF HIGHER LIVING
Atlanta, Georgia

# GOD HAS NOT FORGOTTEN YOU!
## *Now Is The Time*

Requests for information should be addressed to:

INSTITUTE OF HIGHER LIVING PUBLISHERS
P.O. Box 888731
Atlanta, Ga. 30356

---

ISBN  0-9647046-9-2

---

Printed in the United States of America.

# TABLE OF CONTENTS

# DEDICATION

*Woman, Woman, Woman, this book is for you.*

*It's message is a message of love.*

*God has not forgotten you.*

*African queen,*

*Walking the banks of the Congo,*

*Laving your limbs in the Niger,*

*Playing at tag with the Nile,*

*God has not forgotten you.*

*WOMAN of bondage,*

*Being translated as unloved,*

*Thinking of yourself as being despised,*

*Feeling like you are unwanted,*

*God has not forgotten you.*

*WOMAN of strength and endurance,*

*Achieving against all odds,*

*Trying to touch the stars,*

*Striving to capture the light,*

*God has not forgotten you.*

*WOMAN of substance,*

*Christ-centered woman.*

*Beloved of the Almighty God.*

*The beauty of His Strength within,*

*God has not forgotten you.*

*Love is the key, love is redemption;*

*Love is salvation, and love is peace,*

*Joy and righteousness. God is love*

*And those who abide in love*

*Abide in God and God in them.*

*Woman, this book is for you.*

*Its message is a message of love.*

*God has not forgotten you.*

# ACKNOWLEDGMENTS

I wish to acknowledge and thank the many people who have given me spiritual, financial and physical support. Your support and encouragement is greatly appreciated. Thank you Ms. Broussard, Carolyn, Carmelia, Joseph, Gloria M., Tai, Gloria H., Margaret, Candice, Fran, Laura, Marge, Rebecca, Mitch, Beverly  Kim, Lawren, Dr. Neely Chandler and a host of others who  labored in prayer for God's purpose to be fulfilled.

I love and appreciate all of you.

# FOREWORD

Many of us equate living according to the Word of God, with prosperity, healing and freedom from worries and fears. But one thing we overlook is how to live a life that is pleasing to God. That is what Beverly has focused on in all of her writings.

Beverly has gone beyond prosperity, beyond freedom from worries or fears to become an intercessor, a prayer warrior, a "God said it therefore it is settled" type of woman. She deals with living holy before a Holy God as the Word states in 1Peter1:16, "Be ye holy; for I am holy". As we experience holy living, we sometimes feel uncomfortable and think it is impossible to do, because we say "We are human". You are right, it is impossible to live holy, but Jesus said in Matthew 19:26, "With man it is impossible; but with God all things are possible".

*"GOD HAS NOT FORGOTTEN YOU! Now Is The Time"* is the *best* book I have ever read pertaining to the plight of the African American woman. While reading this book, you will begin to see your life from a whole new perspective. If you embrace the principles in this book, I promise you that your life will

be transformed.

"*GOD HAS NOT FORGOTTEN YOU! Now Is The Time*" will educate you. Its poems will inspire you. Its examples will motivate you and the Word of God will deliver you. It is a book to be **read over and over again.** You will be encouraged, motivated and filled with the glory of God because truly "*GOD HAS NOT FORGOTTEN YOU! Now Is The Time*"

Carmelia J. Ervin
Retired Elementary Teacher

# INTRODUCTION

The American household has been faced with many forms of deprivation within the last decade. Economic and social disparity, along with moral corruption, has spread and disintegrated the foundation of American society. New ideas and ways of thinking have challenged the core of the traditional family.

People of all races and cultures in America are experiencing the vast destruction within the society. Many people are suffering great pain, fear, hopelessness, and despair. This horrific dilemma has particularly affected the African American household. Signs of stress and deterioration are everywhere. Swollen welfare rolls, rising divorce rates, immoral living, rising alcohol and drug use, staggering increases in diseases, mental illnesses, and the roster goes on....

Strong forces are at work endeavoring to rob, kill and destroy the family structure. These strong forces of disparity have given rise to increasing dissension within the African American community. Self-destructive machination have infuriated many families to attack and destroy each other en masse.

Sundry contingencies have had a profound effect on the problems that plague the African American household.

1) Slavery and racism have contributed to a large part of the problems that plague African Americans today. Although, the method of the institution has changed, the outcome remains the same;

2) The decline of moral and religious ethics altered the impact of the church. As a result moral values seemed to be a thing of the past;

3) The prison and welfare system have contributed to the removal of African American fathers from the home and created a large group of females as heads of their households.

4) The lack of social privileges such as equal rights, quality education and technological training has caused a large proportion of African Americans to fall into this society's poverty range. These, I believe, are the chief causes of the continual decline of the African American family and deserve to be addressed.

Today the African American woman is assuming more and more leadership roles in her household, as she continues to raise her children without the father in the home. Her household faces destruction on every side. The pressures of life weigh heavily upon her shoulders while she is helplessly being torn apart. She is often ignored and misunderstood. She now finds herself in a state of confusion, disarray, bitterness, anger, and unforgiveness, not knowing how she actually got into this web or how she is going to get out. As she continues to be oppressed by escalating problems in her household, it is obvious that she is suffering beyond measure. Yet, hardly anyone seems to notice or care as she reaches out for help in passive or aggressive means.

It is important for her to be healed, delivered and set free. Many mothers have prayed, suffered and died so that their loved ones could be free from slavery and racism. When we face our problems, value our life and know our purpose for being here, only then can we begin to experience true freedom and enjoy life to its fullest.

This book is written in a manner that will present:

a) The Beginning - the life of African woman;

b) Until Now - the life of the African American woman;

c) The Woman of Substance -the Christ-centered woman. The spiritual consciousness of the African American woman will be enlightened as the Lord moves her in the position of a woman of royal priesthood, holy and loved.

WOMAN! NOW IS THE TIME TO LET YOUR LIGHT SHINE. GOD HAS NOT FORGOTTEN YOU! He desires to heal your wounds and deliver you from past and present bondage that could hinder your chances of eternal life with Him. It is my prayer that upon completion of this book, you the reader,  will know and experience the love of God, the eyes of your understanding will be enlightened and you will  receive greater wisdom, knowledge, and understanding of what God is revealing .

## Chapter One

# IN HIS TIME

At an early age I became aware of the prejudice that was present in this world. Although I never desired to be someone other than myself, I always wanted to be given the opportunity to be the best that I could be. I wanted to be free in the country in which I was born, free to love and to be loved; to give and to receive, to enjoy all the finer things life has to offer. But I continued to hear that I would not be able to reach the goal that I had set for myself.

I would look at the photographs of Jesus, with a white face and blue eyes, and found it to be confusing especially when the bible depicts Him in a different manner. Just one picture can speak a thousand words. Some people might say it is just a point of contact but it is more than that. It represents truth. And children will not look at the photo and say Jesus is a Jew. No, they will say Jesus was a white man. For a group of people who has had such horrific oppression and persecution by the hands of white people, it is understandable why accepting Jesus as Lord and Savior over my life was not easy. To me it was just another way of justifying white is what is holy and righteous and black was just the opposite.

We teach children of all colors about Jesus and I have seen little children of color become even more insecure once they come in contact with the image of a white Jesus. Some actually believe that Jesus will hear the little white children's prayers before He will hear theirs. A white person told a person of color that because they were white, God was going to answer their prayers simply because they were white. The sad part about this lie is that some people believe this to be truth.

Sometimes pictures speak louder than words. The silent prejudice of a simple picture imprinted into a child's mind does speak loudly and can hinder the true Christ from setting up an accurate and solid foundation in the lives of children when they enter adulthood. Therefore, trusting in Jesus as Lord and Savior over my life was not an easy task for me.

How could Jesus be white and allow men to enslave my race of people? Why were blacks so despised, and why were they bound in a free society? The answers to these questions were never made clear to me as a growing child. Blacks seemed to belittle each other and uplift the ones that kept them bound. As I grew older, I continued to see African American families mutilated. Families were together and yet not really together. While negative words continued to be spoken over them, they continued to speak negative words over themselves. I began to question whether there was a God and whether He too, was prejudice. I was determined to hear from God. If He were with me, He would surely reveal Himself to me. I sought after God with all my heart and soul, but still I could not hear Him.

In 1973 the Holy Spirit got my attention. He said, "Jesus loves you. He has not forgotten you! Your peace and joy will come when you know and accept my plan and purpose for your life." I realized that God's timing was not my timing and He was always on time. He wanted me to love Him with all my heart, soul and strength. He wanted all of me. I had to pursue His kind of love at all cost. I agreed to commit my life to Him. Then I heard a still small voice within say, "You must take your parents out of My position. I shall have no other gods before Me."

It took several weeks before I could truthfully place the Lord before my parents in my heart, but finally I was able to be obedient to the Word of God! He will not have any other gods before Him. How I wanted to get to know Him and fellowship with Him! I began to study His word. I believed He wanted to use me to bring healing to His people. How this was going to be accomplished was still unknown to me.

My knowledge of Jesus increased. A greater love for God began to emerge. The Holy Spirit taught me more about Jesus Christ the Son of the living God. I believed that Jesus Christ was the Son of Almighty God, and that He died, was buried, and rose again from the dead so that I could have life everlasting.

I read about Jesus and the image I had of Him began to change. Revelation 1:14, 15 declares that His head and His hair were white like wool, as white as snow; and His eyes were as a flame of fire; and

His feet like unto fine brass as if they burned in a furnace; and his voice as the sound of many waters." That meant that He was mature, full of wisdom, discernment and sound mind. He worked and suffered severely so that I could have His life more abundantly.

Jesus came to save mankind, and God did not curse the Black race but chose them to be His very own. "God so loved the world that He gave His only begotten Son, that whosoever believeth in Him should not perish but have everlasting life." (John 3:16). God sent Jesus so that through Him the world might be saved. So I gladly made Him Lord and Savior over my life. The more I reached out to Him, the more I was able to experience His goodness.

I experienced a greater measure of God's power and love in 1979. I asked the Holy Spirit to come into my heart and help me to become more like Jesus. The Holy Spirit entered my heart by faith and my life was never the same. An instant change inside of me had taken place. I began to thirst for God's Word and the eyes of my understanding were enlightened. Love and joy filled my heart, and the bondage of sin and damnation was broken. I felt as though I could fly, for the burden of sin no longer weighed heavily on my shoulders. God placed in my heart a peace that surpassed all understanding and a joy that was inexpressible. Again I heard that still gentle voice say, "My child, I have not forgotten you!"

As I hid the word of God in my heart, His love grew within me and the burden for the African American family to be made whole increased. God was preparing me to spread the good news about Jesus to my family, country, and to the rest of the world. I was led by the Holy Spirit to develop a workshop on Christian Living. He would awaken me in the early mornings and commune with me through the Word of God.

Soon after the workshop materials were completed, I received a call from Mary, one of my prayer partners, with whom I had shared God's vision for my life. She told me that she had about twenty people that were interested in attending the workshop. At first I was a little hesitant but she assured me that the Lord was making a way for His Word to go forth to His people. I agreed to give the workshop and the results were gloriously triumphant. To my amazement, within the next two weeks sixty people had signed up for the next workshop.

Almighty God revealed to me that He had called me to counsel, teach, and evangelize. The workshop gave me the assurance that He was sending me forth to minister to others in a new and fresh way. Then He gave me one of the most difficult tasks of my life. I was directed by the Holy Spirit to give the workshop to my family. At first I was rather apprehensive, realizing that I was the youngest in the family. But each time I would finish reading the Bible I would get the same message.

The Word of God says that obedience is better than sacrifice. Therefore, in obedience, I began to prepare diligently for the workshop. Like the first workshop, the Lord poured out great blessings upon my family and me. These experiences made me realize that the Lord's ways are not our ways and He will do what He says He will do in His time.

As the workshops continued, I became acutely aware of the condition and plight of the African American woman. The workshop was one of the tools that God used to open my eyes to the state of the souls of mankind. The Holy Spirit began to use me in the area of writing. It gave me such peace to know that God was in the center of my being. Writing did not come to me naturally.

Nonetheless, God used my hands as the pen of a ready writer. Short stories, poems, and sermons came forth overwhelmingly from my heart. One of the poems that came forth was titled "The Beginning Until Now." It vividly portrayed the history of the African American woman. This poem broadened my understanding of the plight of the African American woman and God's plan and purpose for her life. I presented this poem to many women, and heartfelt healing has taken place.

The following poem is presented in its entirety. I pray that the Holy Spirit will lead and guide every reader to the depth of truth and insight contained in this following piece.

Chapter Two

# THE BEGINNING
# UNTIL NOW

*Why do you weep, dear queen?*

*Why is your soul cast down?*

*Tell me, Dear Queen, what has caused you*

*To turn your face from my grace?*


*Oh, kind Sir, it started long ago.*

*I was preparing a hot supper,*

*When suddenly I heard a*

*Terrible scream from my children!*

*I ran to see what was the matter,*

*And I was captured by wicked*

*Men from afar.*


*We were thrown into a cold and dark ship*

*And carried into a strange land, far, away.*

*Many men, women,*

*And even children were killed,*

*While others' hearts could not sustain*

*Such inhumane treatment.*

**24**

*My children and I were separated!*

*My husband, I never saw again.*

*I was given two husbands*

*I never really knew.*

*I've been raped many times*

*In this strange land;*

*I've lost all my worth and dignity.*

*I am torn, worn, confused, abused,*

*And feeling I am of no good use!*

*I've given birth to so many children for these two men,*

*A-n-d I hardly know their names.*


**OH, THIS IS WHY I weep, Kind Sir.**

**This is why my s-o-u-l is cast down.**


*Oh, yes! Their names! Master is one,*

*And Slave is the other.*

*Many times while I am working*

*I must stop to be raped*

*By my master husband.*

*Oh, what shame and defilement!*

*What a terrible spirit of whoredom, cruelty,*

*Fear and deceitfulness that was placed upon me!*

*There have been times when I was asleep*

*With my slave husband,*

*And my master husband awakened me*

*And raped me! I had no one to rescue me*

*From this cycle of sin and damnation.*

**OH, THIS IS WHY I weep, Kind Sir.**

**This is why M-y soul is cast down.**

*I was forced to live in a vicious cycle*

*Of sin in this strange land.*

*Marred, beaten, raped, defiled, shamed,*

*Stolen, robbed, unprotected,*

*I was prey for all to pounce upon and crush.*

*My children began to fall into the pattern*

*Of the life-style of this strange land.*

*Now some are for the master*

*And some are for the slave.*

*A-n-d I hardly know their names.*

**OH, THIS IS WHY I weep, Kind Sir.**

**This is why M-Y SOUL is cast down.**

*One day, out of desperation,*

*I cried to my slave husband,*

*"Help me regain my position that*

*I had back home!*

*Please fight to protect me!*

*Preserve my dignity, I plead!"*

*But he turned to me and said,*

*"I shall not fight for you! I'm afraid;*

*I don't want to die!*

*And why should I protect you?*

*I have no attachment to you!*

*And besides, Master has trained me to*

*Abuse and misuse you as he does.*

*So why don't you continue*

*To jump and shout anyhow?"*

**OH, THIS IS WHY I weep, Kind Sir.**

**This is why MY SOUL is cast down.**

*I cried to my master husband, begging him*

*To acknowledge my position as queen*

*And give me back my dignity.*

*I pleaded with him to allow me*

*To train our daughters*

*To have one husband that would love*

*And protect them.*

*To train our sons to love and protect*

*The sanctity of their women.*

*He just laughed and laughed and laughed,*

*"When will you ever learn, girl,*

*That this thing called integrity*

*Is not something we practice.*

*It is only something to talk about."*

*I begged him to repent and to remove the spirit*

*Of whoredom from the midst of our children.*

*But he only lashed my back and raped me*

*Again and again and again, forcing me to be*

*Obedient To his lustful and irrational demands.*


**OH, THIS IS WHY I weep, Kind Sir.**

**This is why my s-o-u-l is cast down.**


*"Kind Sir, why are you still here!*

*Why have you not left me?*

*How can you look at me with*

*So much love and tenderness?*

My master husband says "Your  black,

*Unlovable, mean, and cruel ".*

*Yet you see me as  precious and valuable.*

*You are the only one who can remove the spirit*

*Of whoredom from  my children and me.*

*Will protect us and give us back our dignity?*

*Will you remove sin and damnation from the*

*Midst of my children, so they can live*

*In eternity with You?"*

**YES, KIND SIR, WE WILL BE YOURS.**

**I SURRENDER MY LIFE TO YOU FOREVER.**

"You will give my girls a husband,

Who will love and appreciate them.

You will reverse this curse

That has been placed upon

My children and me.

You will give them the freedom to live holy

And victorious in this strange land."

**YES, KIND SIR, WE WILL BE YOURS.**

**I SURRENDER MY LIFE TO YOU FOREVER.**

But her children began to turn

From the Lord God Almighty.

They turned from pursuing

Righteousness to ways of wickedness,

And they adopted the life-styles

Of this strange and adulterous world.

**30**

*They made their master and material*

*Things their gods.*

*They forgot about the Almighty God.*

*They strove to be like the one*

*That had enslaved them!*


**OH, THEY LEFT THEIR FIRST LOVE!**

**THEY LEFT THE LIVING AND TRUE GOD!**


*They became vain in their imaginations,*

*Hearers of the Word but not doers.*

*They became lovers of themselves.*

*Covetous, boastful, proud, blasphemous,*

*Disobedient to parents, ungrateful, unholy,*

*Preferring good times to worshipping God,*

*And having a form of godliness*

*But denying the power thereof.*

*Their sins will not only destroy their lives*

*On earth, but also make them hell-bound.*

*NOW, why do you weep, dear queen?*

*Why are you so deeply distressed?*

*Tell me, what has caused you*

*To turn to everyone but me?*

*Why have you left Me?*

**I AM YOUR FIRST LOVE!**

**WELL, KIND SIR...**

*It was lack of knowledge, understanding and Godly wisdom that has caused us to turn from you, our Deliverer and our First Love.*

MY BELOVED, HUMBLE YOURSELVES, PRAY, REPENT, TURN FROM EVIL, SEEK MY FACE, RETURN TO ME AND BE HOLY, PURE AND UPRIGHT BEFORE ME AND I WILL HEAL, DELIVER, AND SET YOU FREE!

# Chapter Three

# "THE BEGINNING"

## THE AFRICAN WOMAN

*O*n the beginning of the poem we have seen how the African woman is suddenly captured and taken away by force to a far away country. She was removed from her country, her culture, her husband, her children, her relatives, her friends, her comfort and brought to a new land only to live under the most vicious cycle of sin and condemnation. She must have felt extremely valueless and burdened in her heart as she laid, stripped, naked, frightened and in great physical and emotional pain.

She and her people were stacked on top of each other in a wet, cold, dark and dreary ship. Imagine, how encumbered and disorientated she must have been as she laid polluted in her own blood, urine and feces for days, weeks and months. Oh, what a tormenting experience this must have been for the African woman.

One day she was a lady with a future, culture, family and purpose. Then in a blink of an eye, the right to life was snatched from her. That alone was traumatic enough, but this was only the beginning of a non-ending, destructive horror with no rest for the weary soul of the African woman. No longer was she considered a human being. She was forced to live as if she were dead.

How detrimental it must have been for her, stripped, branded, trapped and standing there in fear-ful hysteria as she watched her whole world savagely snatched from her. I don't believe her mind was able to grasp the dynamics of what was happening. She was a woman who had feelings. She was a gentle, loving, kind, and emotional soul now deprived of even thinking for herself. She was stripped of all rights given by God to all human beings. This in itself was enough to crush her soul! Yet, it was only the beginning of a never-ending, savage horror.

Instantaneously, she found herself thrown into an auction line and sold as a commodity. She was treated like an animal and in some instances her meals were served in the same manner as the animals. She was forced to live under this condition day after day, month after month and year after year. Soon ten years went by, 30, 50, 60 years and still she lived under the same conditions. More devastating for her was to give birth to children and watch them live under such hardship and pain.

The horror she faced never, never, never seemed to end. Soon she became defiled and abused by the master and his slave whom in many instances, she did not even know or relate to. One reason for this is that many African men and women belonged to different tribal groups and spoke different languages.

Many times the master purposely placed them together. By not understanding the language of her white or black abusers, she lacked the ability to express her thoughts and emotions fully. Neither was she allowed to do so. Therefore, she was denied the satisfaction of freely enjoying the right to love and be loved. Her nightmares were unending. Living a life of constant fear, brutal oppression, being raped repeatedly, and never given the freedom to experience love and affection, no doubt, robbed her of all rights given to every human being. She was forced to live a life of whoredom, fornication, bondage and oppression. She had no controlled her life nor the life of her children. They were force to live under sexual exploitation as well as other kinds of defilement. As time went by she became conditioned to daily abuse as a way of life for her and her children.

One aspect of this horror that has seldom been addressed is the detrimental and deadly effect rape had upon the African American woman. Rape is a vicious act of violence. Its purpose is to dominate or degrade and finally destroy its victim. Survivors of this violent crime usually continue to suffer emotionally.

The soul (the seat of emotions) of a person is extremely delicate, and such defilement causes big scars. Unless the woman comes to know the healing power of Jesus, it is possible to be bruised beyond medical repair. We can't begin to understand the devastating effect rape had upon the African woman. The Bible gives a man the penalty of death as the punishment for such a harmful crime. This sin was so vicious and destructive it still affects the life of the African American woman today. Because of lack of knowledge, she continues to reap the harvest of the sexual perversions that took place hundreds of years ago.

The after effect of rape may cause its victim to feel angry, fearful, ashamed, helpless, trapped and unclean. At times, she is even unable to sleep. Her sexual intimacy is hindered. In most cases that I have read and encountered the trauma is so destructive, the woman usually find it difficult to resume normal relationships with others. It must have been an even more traumatic experience for the African woman. She was prohibited to reach out to anyone for comfort or support. Even minimal means of communicating her feelings were stripped from her.

Most of the people around her spoke different languages. Along with the many other depravity she is molested repeatedly. I know of no other group of women who have been defiled is such a hideous and morbid ways. She was raped in every aspect of her life-physically, emotionally, psychologically, mentally and spiritually. This became a way of life for her in America.

The African woman and her children were trained to live under such degrading conditions month after month and year after year. Most women trained to live under such conditions and circumstances no doubt would lose their moral integrity, self respect and possibly their very soul. When a woman is raped in America today, there are usually counselors who attempt to rehabilitate her to a state of wholeness. Even then the healing never totally takes place. Oh, what pain it must still be for the African American woman who has never had anyone to nurse her back to a state of health and well-being!

Never has any other group of women in America been exploited as the African American woman. Yet, she continues to thrive against all odds. Faith in God kept her alive. She had a vision of freedom and never lost sight of one day being free to love, be loved, and enjoy the rights that were sadistically taken from her.

She can be heard singing " AMAZING GRACE," "BYE AND BYE," "THE LORD WILL MAKE A WAY," "SWING LOW," "NOBODY KNOWS THE TROUBLE I'VE SEEN." She has never let go of faith and hope that one day God would redeem her and make her free indeed forevermore. Woman! Now Is The Time. He loves and cares for you. His plan and purpose for your life is for good and not for evil. It is vital that you know His plan and purpose for your life. If you are to be victorious through out the new millennium, you must grow into the knowledge of the Word of God.

Chapter Four

# UNTIL NOW

*THE AFRICAN AMERICAN WOMAN*

After giving birth to children that were born of the master and the slave, the African woman had biracial children which produced a race of people with varied shades of color. Those who were the children of the master (lighter hue) were treated a little better than the rest of the slaves (darker hue).

These children with varies shades of color were called Negroes in the beginning. Later the name was changed to Colored people and now they are referred to as Blacks/African Americans. Although her children did not share many of her earlier experiences, they still had devastating experiences of their own. Their daily life continue to be filled with grotesque and startling despair since the arrival of the former slaves brought to the Americas by ship. Despite these conditions, the desire to be free was deeply embedded within the heart of the old and the young.

The African American woman was thrown into a world that placed barriers at every step of the way to ensure failure. Freedom was given on paper, but in reality she was still treated as a slave. Her wounds were deep with scars digging at the very core of her being.

She yearned for love and acceptance. Yet, racism did not give her the privilege of enjoying peace and tranquility. Faced with ongoing forms of ruthless treatment and having no one to comfort her, she  choose to mask the pain, which caused her to sink deeper into despair and loneliness. Through God's grace, the African American woman finally received some aspects of freedom. This freedom came from the Bible which gave her directions on how to live. She had cried out to man for help, but to no avail. She soon discovered that when she cried out to the Lord God Almighty, He delivered her. Joyously and with renewed hope, the African American woman pursued a better life for herself and her family.

Abraham Lincoln's intention was not to free the slaves. Signing the emancipation proclamation did not entirely free the slave either. I believe it was the prayers of the slave fathers and  mothers that reached heaven and God heard their cry. God freed her and her people so that they could freely serve and worship Him.

He wanted the African American woman to live a holy and upright life. He wanted to remove the toxic, lewd, immoral, lustful, promiscuous, and malicious life-style that was venomously placed upon her. This is why it was vital for her to use the Bible to direct her way of living.

Eagerly, she and her family continued tenaciously in pursuit of their education. Throughout their struggles in the free world, developing skills for better economic opportunities increasingly became their priority. Unfortunately, as time past the African American woman and her family lost sight of the importance of putting God first in their life and using the Bible as a way of living. The church evolved more and more as a social gathering for releasing tension. And the emphasis shifted away from honoring God and obeying His laws. Instead, their focus was on a better life in this society and to be accepted by man in hopes that racism and oppression would be destroyed. But the evils of sin through prejudice, bigotry, and oppression increased standing in the way of their progress. During the course of their development, African Americans did experience great victories. However, looking to man instead of God, resulted in many defeats and setbacks. The loss of integrity, togetherness, moral soundness, love for one another, and a holy and chaste life contributed to their downfall. Still worst of all, they left their first love.

Today many African American women are living under the horrible bondage of welfare. In many instances the bondage of welfare is like slavery since it defiles and strips them of respect and value. This system promises so much help but only with compromises that promote a life-style of sin and poverty for the African American woman. She is caught up in the web of raising her children without the assistance of a husband. Helplessly, she has succumbed to another form of slavery. Now in the African American household single parent families seem to be the norm.

Many African American women are still married

to Uncle Sam while many of the African American men are still married to the prison system. Further separation results from increased dependencies on drugs and alcohol. These evil tactics, which weaken and destroy, continue to defile and enslave African American family. They have been trained to live under these conditions for such a long time that now they are considered the norm. Incarceration and unemployment of African American men have caused a devastating decline in their responsibility, protection and love for African American women.

There are African American women who are well established financially but do not have stable, respectable relationships with the opposite sex. Many enjoy a life without male companionship, while others have accepted living with men who are not their husbands or sharing other women's husbands. Still a growing number of women are involved in lesbian relationships. And there are still some women who have managed to keep their marriages together even though they have wrestled with constant infidelity. Some have been blessed with godly men who truly love and respect them. These are women who have overcome the odds since they are one with God and one with their husbands.

But can more African American women and their families survive the gruesome ordeal they now face? God is and has the answer to that question. He will reveal His plan to all that have an ear to hear.

## ALMIGHTY GOD SPEAKS

Almighty God is speaking to you my sister. He has not forgotten you. Now Is The Time! Open your heart and let the Holy Spirit bring healing unto you. Throughout your life and the life of your people, great suffering, pain and sorrow have you known. Most people don't see your pain or know how fragile you really are. They are not aware of your need to be loved, handled gently, understood and protected. Your heavenly Father has seen your pain and has heard your cry. Your Time is now!

Many of you are still experiencing oppression, racism and poverty. The evil one will continues to try to demean and discredit you, using different manipulative tactics to control your mind. Only when you turn completely to Jesus can He fill you with His love and purpose. Learn of God's plan and purpose for your life is what will give you the love and joy that you seek. Remember! Only Jesus can deliver you. He wants to establish healthy relationships in your life. You are called to be a disciple of Christ. You must understand that apart from Christ you can do nothing.

My daughter, I, the Lord, was there when evil men defiled the younger girls as well as the older women. The evil one came and still comes to steal, kill, and destroy. Though completely entangled, inwardly and outwardly, you can still be delivered and set free through the shed blood of Jesus Christ.

The evils of slavery may have caused you to lose your self-respect, your self-worth, exclusive rights to your body and rights to freedom; indeed you could have lost the very essence of your being. I was there! I was the one who carried you through. You were bruised beyond measure, yet I knew you and came to your rescue. You will now cease from being tortured and I am your peace. Listen, listen, listen I heard your cry and your plea. I gave you visions and dreams that you must hold on to and keep the faith. For too long have you suffered from the lack of rest, concentration, genuine love, knowledge and application of My Word. Now, I have come to set you totally free. Only through Jesus can you be saved and set free; and he whom the Son sets free is free indeed. Daughters of Zion know that I am the Truth, the Way, and the Life. Only through Me can you be saved, delivered and set free." Thus saith the Lord.

Romans 10:9-11 states, "That if thou shall confess with thy mouth the Lord Jesus, and shall believe in thine heart that God raised Him from the dead, thou shall be saved. For with the heart, man believeth unto righteousness; and with the mouth, confession is made unto salvation." The Scripture also says, "Whosoever believeth on Him shall not be ashamed." To those reading this book, I employ you to believe and receive Jesus inside your heart. He will heal and deliver you from all unrighteousness.

The love of Jesus is unconditional. He sees your value when no one else can see it. He desires to give you that peace which passes all understanding. Do not seek for love and peace in this world. The world does not have love and peace to give. Only through Christ can you receive the love and peace you have been searching for. Jesus has sent the Holy Spirit to lead, guide, and protect you from the entanglement of sin and damnation.

You have God's blueprint (Bible) on how to raise your children and lead a life filled with His kind of love. Real freedom comes from within. Do not continue to imitate the life-styles of those that are not laid out in the Bible. Only as you follow Christ can you see the light and be free. Your guide to living is mapped out for you in His Word. In the world you will never, never, never, find peace because there is no peace. Only in the Kingdom of the Almighty God can you experience everlasting peace.

The African American woman has lived in bondage too long. She continues to run to man for affirmation and love instead of returning to her First Love. In the hundreds of years of conditioning and entangling herself again and again in the life-styles of this world, she has found no peace. She must now leave the wilderness and by faith enter into the Promised Land. She must be BORN AGAIN! There is no peace if she does not face her past and present state of bondage and choose to return to the Almighty God in word and in truth. Avoiding the past and present will only keep her in bondage.

Almighty God has heard her cry and her plea and has shown her the way to receive true and lasting freedom. God gave her His only begotten Son and if she would dare to believe and receive Him as Lord and Savior over her life she would be saved. Take on a new life and let the joy of the Lord be your strength. Arm yourself with faith, hope and love. You were placed here so that His kind of love and faith could be manifested on earth through you. Remember! He freed the African American woman and her family once they asked for forgiveness, repented, humbled themselves, turned from their evil ways, and made Jesus Lord and Savior over their lives. Now you can let His kind of love mature within you so that you can spread His gospel all around the world! Now is the time.

"I have not left you, says the Lord! You have left Me, your First Love. You have been practicing the life-style of this world. You no longer revere My Word. Return to Me. Stop letting the cares of this world, the pride of life, and the lust of the flesh consume you. Begin walking by faith. Honor, praise and worship Me. I am a jealous God and I will have no other gods before Me. Having a form of godliness, but denying the power thereof, will only move you further and further away from Me."

Will the African American woman and her family survive? Will they repent? Will they return to God and live? Now is the time for God's plan to go forth in their lives! Will they again be saved from eternal damnation?

In the poem "The Beginning Until Now," Jesus spoke with love, power and might to the African American woman. She was stolen and brought to this country and sold. It was only through Jesus that she could be delivered and set free. He saw her value when no one else could see it. She faced hardships that were very different from those of other Americans. The oppression, daily pressures and responsibilities of life weighed heavily upon her shoulders. Instead of seeking Jesus for help, she continued to turn to man (to those who are enslaved themselves). Yet His hand is stretched out still as He yearns for her to repent, ask for forgiveness, turn from evil, make Him Lord and Savior over her life and live in obedience to His Word.

All have sinned and fallen short of the glory of God. The African American woman must acknowledge (like all who become Christians) she has sinned and ask God for forgiveness. Now you must repent and ask Jesus to be Lord and Savior over your life. Believe on the name of Jesus and be delivered from eternal damnation. The Lord has sent His Holy Spirit to lead, to guide, and to protect His children from the entanglement of sin. He is still calling the African American woman to a life filled with love, holiness, peace, joy and prosperity.

As seen in the poem, the Lord also gave the woman a blueprint on how to raise her children. He commanded her to be born again and to follow the biblical principle according to the Holy Scriptures. But instead of obeying God, her children began to practice the customs of the world. They turned from the true and living God. The cares of this world, the pride of life, the lust of the flesh consumed them. They no longer strive to walk by faith and praise Him with a holy life-style. They had a form of godliness, but denied the power thereof. God is a God of a second chance! He has had mercy on the African American woman and has given her new songs to sing in this hour. He is fulfilling His plan and purpose for her life. If your spirit is in agreement grab hold and never let go of this truth. If God's children do not accept His word now, they will continue to destroy one another en masse. What can stop God's blessing to come forth among His people? If you turn your back on Jesus, not accepting the position that comes through justification and the demonstration that comes through sanctification. The problem is many people today love to live in darkness better than they love to live in the light.

When you set your eyes gazing at others who enjoy the evils of this world, you too may succumb to the lust of the eyes and the pride of life. Listen, listen, listen, and take heed the Lord is speaking!

*Being filled with all unrighteousness, fornication, wickedness, covetousness, maliciousness; full of envy, murder, debate, deceit, malignity;*

**49**

*whisperers,*

*Backbiters, haters of God, despiteful, proud, boasters, inventors of evil things, disobedient to parents,*

*Without understanding, covenant breakers, without natural affection, implacable, unmerciful:*

*Who knowing the judgment of God, that they which commit such things are worthy of death, not only do the same, but have pleasure in them that do them.*

*Romans 1:29-32*

*Even as Sodom and Gomorrah, and the cities about them in like manner, giving themselves over to fornication, and going after strange flesh, are set forth for an example, suffering the vengeance of eternal fire*

*(Jude 1:7).*

*But I have a few things against thee, because thou hast there them that hold the doctrine of Balaam, who taught Balac to cast a stumbling block before the children of Israel, to eat things sacrificed unto idols, and to commit fornication*

*(Revelation 2:14).*

*Notwithstanding I have a few things against thee, because thou sufferest that woman Jezebel, which*

*calleth herself a prophetess, to teach and to se-
duce my servants to commit fornication, and to
eat things sacrificed unto idols*

*(Revelation 2:20).*

*And I gave her space to repent of her fornication;
and she repented not. Revelation 9:21 Neither repented they of their murders, nor of their sorcer-
ies, nor of their fornication, nor of their thefts*

*(Revelation 2:21).*

God is speaking to you, African American woman,
turn from world, turn to Him and began living holy
and upright lives at all cost! Call on the name of
Jesus and be set free from sin and damnation. You
will never experience peace, joy, and eternal life if
you continue to pursue the ways of darkness which
lead to eternal damnation.

The African American woman is known to have
achieved greatness in spite of her setbacks, fears,
pain and grief yet what she really desires is to have
real love and peace within. Her pain and grief have
been passed down from generation to generation leav-
ing her with a bleeding heart. She longs for someone to reach out and snatch her from this horrible
bondage.

Deep within many still cling to God in hopes that
one day He will rescue them and allow them to en-

joy love peace and joy in this world and the world to come. Will she and her family turn to the living God? Only God knows the answer to that question, and He will reveal the answer to her if she opens her heart and mind to hear His Word. She must first accept Jesus into her heart and let His kind of love rule and reign within. Will she choose to follow the blueprint to salvation and live? Will she answer "yes" to the call of God? I pray she will.

## Chapter Five

# WILL

# SHE SURVIVE?

$\mathcal{T}$he African American woman must make a choice to continue to live in bondage or be set free by the shed blood of Jesus Christ. She was taught to believe that having black skin meant that she was evil, wicked, dirty, and ugly. Now she must learn the truth to be free indeed. There are many white, yellow, red and black people with ungodly hearts that God considers evil ugly dirty and wicked. It is not the color of the skin that validates a person's worth, but it is the content of the heart. God looks at the heart. Anyone focusing on skin color will continue to be confused and abused by the evil one.

The Lord Jesus desires the African American woman to be His Bride. He is not looking at her skin. He is looking at her spirit and soul. God looks at her heart. He has been with her through the horrors of her mental, physical, emotional and spiritual abuse. God knows that she has been robbed of healthy family relationships. Yet, through God's grace and mercy she survived it. Now she must continue to live in Christ for only through Christ can she live a victorious life. God will turn her mourning into joy. He has a plan and purpose for her life. The devil tried to keep the victor's cup from her, but now she knows the truth, will face the truth and the truth will make her free.

The African American woman and her family are in some ways similar to Joseph in Genesis, Chapters 37-50. Joseph had a dream, and neither he nor his family understood the dream. Jealousy was the reaction from his brothers, and they proceeded to get rid of him. The devil is the one behind all evil. He tried to use many people to destroy Joseph so God's plans would not be fulfilled. But Joseph held on to the dream even though he didn't fully understand it. He survived because he had absolute faith in God; he continued to forgive and to love those who had falsely accused and misused him. Those that the devil had used to try to destroy Joseph were the ones to whom he brought deliverance. So it is with the African American woman. She is called to turn from unrighteousness and turn to living a holy and upright life. Only then will God's plan be fulfilled.

In the past, many looked down on her. She became an outcast. But God placed His grace, His mercy, and His love upon her, giving her a chance to come into right standing with Him. She will no longer be disgraced or live in fear and shame. When you are a new creature, old things are passed away and all things become new. Almighty God is her Redeemer! In the past she was abandoned, but now with His great compassion, God is drawing her nearer to Him. With everlasting love He will show her His salvation.

God is pouring out His anointing on the African American woman and her family who repent and turn to Him. God is showing forth His love and power in their lives for His purpose. God's plan and purpose for her life will be revealed. The African American woman who turns to Jesus will develop new and loving relationships with Him and others. She must not have any other gods before Him. Unity and love will spring forth from her. Peace and love will be hers forever. God has called the African American woman to live a life of holiness, love, and forgiveness, growing in grace, and maturing in pray. And for all who have crushed her soul forgive them, Lord for they know not what they do! The African American woman and her family are extremely vital to the body of Christ. God is bringing His family together in love and unity and trusting them to build His kingdom here on earth. This can only be accomplished through obedient souls.

Will she and her family survive? Yes! Rather than looking to man for help, she must realize that her help comes from the Lord God Almighty and turn to him for her soul salvation. Only then she will surely walk in victory. The Lord must be the center of her life. All who are born again, walking in obedience to the will of God, will not only survive, but triumph! Now is the time for God's will to be manifested in her life.

Chapter Six

# TRANSFORMED FROM THE OLD TO THE NEW

*W*hen we repent of our sins and turn to God, we become a new creature. Our spirits come alive and we no longer live the life of the world. We are in the world but not of the world. We begin to live in the Kingdom of God and our total being changes. True repentance will bring about a change. The old life that was filled with wickedness we will detest and begin to discard all that is not connected to his new nature.

David, a man after God's own heart, said that he would hide God's word in his heart so that he would not sin against God. God has outlined for us the sins that bring death and recognizing sin helps us avoid them. When you gave your life to Christ, old things passed away and all things became new. Why? Because you have been transferred from the kingdom of darkness to the Kingdom of light, from the kingdom of sin to the Kingdom of righteousness.

Below are some of the manifestation in the life of sinners. This list will help you know what to discard and what not to imitate. By studying the nature of sin, you will gain more insight into the kingdom of darkness. You are by no means limited only to the ones mentioned below. As you mature in the Word, the Holy Spirit will teach you more.

*OLD LIFE*

- Some manifestations of the old life are:

- 1. Rage - wrath, bitterness, anger, irritation.

- 2. Pride - vanity, conceit, pride, swelled - head, boasting, self-glorification, vain-glory, arrogance, prestige.

- 3. Attention seeking - wanting recognition wanting notice, love of power, controlling/ ruling over others.

- 4. Disobedience - defiance, resistance, discontent, disregard, lack of discipline.

- 5. Hypocrisy - imitation, deceit, lip service.

- 6. Lukewarmness - indifference.

- 7. Anxiety - worry, strain, tension,

- 8. Condemning - judging, convicting,

- criticizing, punishing.

- 9. Unbelief - discouragement, atheism, lack of faith, disbelief, heresy.

- 10. Disrespect - impoliteness, ridicule, dishonor, insulting, mocking.

- 11. Gluttony - overeating, Craving, greediness, indulgence.

- 12. Lying - falsehood, fabrication.

- 13. Gossip - talkativeness, empty talk.

- 14. Lust - eros, sexual desires, adultery, fornication, impurity, carnal passion, abnormality.

*Circle the fruit of the Old Life you want to renounce. They are strongholds that will hinder your walk with the Lord.*

These are the manifestations of the old nature. All of us come into this world with a sinful nature and that is why we must be redeemed and given a new nature. Almighty God offers forgiveness to those who turn from sin to Him. Sin hardens the heart, is destructive, brings reproach, causes misery and leads to poverty. It is worthless and the wages of sin is death.

NEW LIFE

When you accept Christ Jesus into your life and ask the Holy Spirit to take complete control over you, your understanding is enlightened and He begins to teach you the purpose of your calling on this earth. You have been bought with a price. You are in right standing with God. Your whole life has started over. The Holy Spirit begins to teach you and groom you for your position in Heaven. You begin to develop a stronger spiritual foundation daily.

When you are first born again, you are spiritually immature. You must be fed with God's word daily. If you are not fed with God's Word, your faith will not grow and you will continue to live under the dictates of the devil. You will not have peace, joy and fulfillment in this kingdom if you do not study to show yourself approved and hide the Word of God in your heart . Your body becomes the temple of God. Jesus sits at the seat of your heart. It must be kept holy and pure. Practice keeping your body under subjection and use the Bible as a guide for holy living. You may be older and physically, psychologically and emotionally mature, but this new life calls for spiritual maturity. Spiritual maturity calls for daily prayer and communion with God Almighty (Figure 1).

How would you feel going into God's Temple on the Sabbath where smoking, drinking, drugs, fornication, adultery, jealousy and etc., were permitted? You may not want to attend such a temple. You may also view this as an abomination before God. Well, you would not be out of order if you left that temple, for that is what the Holy Spirit does when sin enters our temple. God's Temple is not the building you visit to worship. When you accept Jesus as Lord and Savior over your life, God's Temple resides within you (Figure 2).

Your body is the Temple of God. It is where the Holy Spirit dwells, not the building you visit on the Sabbath. *1Corinthians 6:19-20 (Amplified Bible) states, "Do you not know that your body is the Temple (the very*

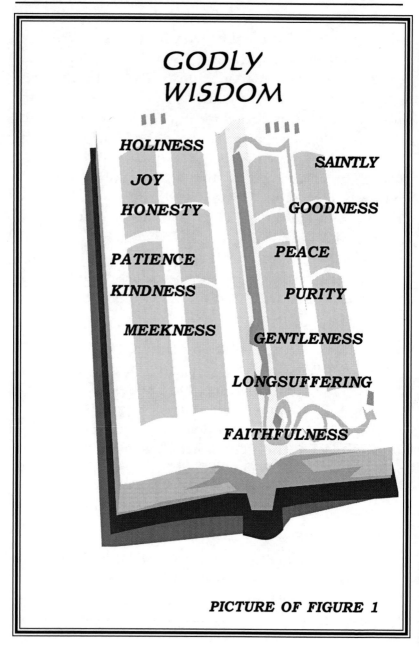

GODLY WISDOM

HOLINESS

SAINTLY

JOY

HONESTY

GOODNESS

PATIENCE

PEACE

KINDNESS

PURITY

MEEKNESS

GENTLENESS

LONGSUFFERING

FAITHFULNESS

PICTURE OF FIGURE 1

PICTURE OF FIGURE 2

*sanctuary) of the Holy Spirit who lives within you, whom you have received [as a Gift] from God? You are not your own. You were bought with a price [purchased with preciousness, paid for, and made His own.]" So honor God and bring glory to Him in your body.* If you continue to sin in your body, you will grieve the Holy Spirit. He does not live in an unclean temple. You must keep your body under subjection and use the Bible as a guide for holy living.

Great value is attached to your spirit, soul and body. Your spirit is alive and your mind must be renewed daily. The Almighty God deposits His kind of love, wisdom, knowledge, and understanding into your heart as you are being transformed into His image and likeness. Now you are ready to represent Him on earth. The Holy Spirit will teach and guides you into the ways of living in the Kingdom of God. Remember He is your teacher.

The nature of the new life is the fruit of the spirit. It is found in *Galatians 5:22-23;" But the fruit of the (Holy) Spirit, [the work which His presence within accomplishes] — is love, joy (gladness), peace, patience (an even temper, forbearance), kindness, goodness (benevolence), faithfulness; 23 (Meekness, humility, gentleness, self-control (self-restraint, continence). Against such things there is no law [that can bring a charge]. "*

Nothing is better than the fruit of the Spirit in the life of a holy being. Those who belong to Jesus have crucified their flesh (old nature) with its passions, appetites and desires [moral corruption]. You will lack for nothing once you learn how to live and move and have your being in the Kingdom of God. God's Word will bring love, peace, joy and happiness to your soul. It will become new, born again, redeemed and restored. You will be reinstated into the Kingdom of Go d Almighty and live with Him for eternity.

The fruit of love is strong and forceful. Once manifested in your life, you will begin to love yourself and others. Seek first the designs, rules, and regulations of God's Kingdom and you will have no lack.

In this world of turmoil, it takes faith to believe and stand firm on your decision to walk in God's love. So make it a point of duty to build on your holy faith. Remember to:

- 1. Study the Bible consistently (II Tim. 2:15).

- 2. Renew your mind daily as you meditate on the      Word (II Cor.4:16).

- 3. Examine yourself to see if you are you glorifying God with your words and deeds, and nor exalting your own selfish desires (II Cor. 13:5).

- 4. Refrain from grieving the Holy Spirit by listening to Him and letting Him guide you in all the affairs of your new life (Eph. 4:30).

- 5. Spend time each day with God in prayer, for that is where your strength lies (1John3:22).

- 6. Fellowship with other Christians and attend a house of worship (John 4:23, 24).

- 7. Apply the Word of God in your life daily, and be a hearer and doer of the Word (James 1:22, 23).

Some manifestations of the new nature that will take root in your life are as follows:

| | |
|---|---|
| Balance | Moral |
| Integrity | Obedience |
| Selflessness | Abstinence |
| Liberty | Cheerfulness |
| Beauty | Perseverance, |
| Decisiveness | Joy |
| Steadfastness | Goodness |
| Courage | Fair-mindedness |
| Watchfulness | Decision |

| | |
|---|---|
| Diligence | Morality |
| Purity | Gracefulness |
| Faith | Self-denial |
| Longsuffering | Meekness |
| Love | Peace |
| Gentleness | Chastity |
| Humility | Loyalty |
| Honesty | Mercifulness |
| Assurance | Compassion |
| Forgiveness | Wisdom |
| Tenderness | Holiness |
| Consecration | Modesty |

*\* Circle the fruit of the New Life maturing within you.*

GOD HAS NOT FORGOTTEN YOU! YOUR TIME IS NOW. Almighty God is calling you to a life of holiness, love, joy, peace, and life everlasting with Him. Do not hold back. Let Him see His image in you! Begin to imitate Jesus in everything you say and do. Oh, how He loves you! He will not allow you to live a defeated life anymore. He will be a defense for you. Your seeds that are holy will live and not perish. Your rights are all in Jesus who will fight and defend you. He will protect you and provide for you and your family. He is Lord and Savior over your life. He yearns for you and will never cease to pray on your behalf to the Father God Almighty. NEVER again shall you be called the forsaken one; your new name will be GOD'S DELIGHT and HIS BRIDE for the Lord delights in you and claims you as HIS OWN.

Chapter Seven

# WOMAN OF

# SUBSTANCE

## THE CHRIST-CENTERED WOMAN

*For my thoughts are not your thoughts, Neither your ways my ways saith the Lord (Isaiah 55:8).*

*N*ow is the time for the Christ-centered woman who is a woman of substance to emerge. In this hour, a woman with a fresh and noble kind of love that guides her character and conduct is about to unfold. She must be enveloped with the strength and protection of Almighty God. This graceful, patient and honest woman will win her family and others to Christ by her gentle and peaceful spirit, which reflects a purity of heart and god fearing nature. She has an inward ageless beauty that is priceless in the sight of God.

This woman of substance has become God's sanctuary through the shed blood of Jesus Christ who washed away her sins. He has covered her with His anointing, beautified her with salvation, clothed her with His righteousness and crowned her with His glory. She has been tested and found to be faithful to God and of a pure heart. Her fruitful vine has been grafted into the branches of the Tree of Life. What a mighty vessel of honor!

The Lord has given her a peaceful mind and a joyful heart. She is prosperous in everything she does and is blessed beyond measure. Her life is filled with prayer and fasting, praise and worship, and giving of thanks. She follows after chastity and purity with patience and humility of heart. She will always be fruitful because she lives a holy, consecrated, and Christ committed life. She rejoices in the hope of the glory of God and He blesses anyone who blesses her.

She conquers evil by doing good. Jesus has exalted her because of her humility. She is loved, respected, and admired by her fellow laborers in Christ. She obeys the Lord Almighty by faithfully keeping all His commandments. Her very being radiates His peace as she gracefully adorns herself with the fruit of the Spirit. She listens with an open heart and has a teachable spirit. Gentleness, kindness, compassion and wisdom speak loudly through her as she spreads the good news of Christ Jesus, her Lord and Savior.

She is a woman of destiny, vision and purpose who has totally surrendered in obedience to God. She ministers to the poor, brokenhearted, imprisoned, blind and battered. Many people will come out of the pit of deception, drugs, alcohol, abuse, sexual promiscuity, and every evil work through her preaching, teaching and living the salvation message. She is truly a beautiful vessel shaped by the Potter's hand to do His Will. Honor, praise and worship are continually in her mouth. She is God's anointed.

There is a common thread that is seen in the great women of the Bible and the Christ-centered women of today. Let us take a look at several women of Biblical influence:

A. Deborah - Means "Bee"

After the death of Joshua, the Lord God raises up judges to lead and rule Israel. Deborah was Israel's only woman judge (Judges 4:5). The Lord chose and used her to do His will. She was respected as a prophetess and judge and recognized as the mother of Israel. As judge, she advised Israel, settled disputes, planned a military strategy against their enemy and led an army into a victorious battle. Deborah was never proud or bitter and did not hold grudges. A godly attitude like Deborah's will promote you and take you to greater heights.

Her husband respected her as well. She wore the hat of prophetess, judge, poet, warrior, and wife without letting these activities come in conflict with her marriage. We can surely call her a virtuous woman as described in Proverb 31. When God is involved in a life there is always unity. What made Deborah more noticeable and respected than the other judges was not that she was a woman but that she was self-denying, humble and obedient to God. Faith, wisdom, strength and courage are other fruits that the Father instills in all whom He calls and uses. He gives us whatever is needed to fulfill the task.

God has called, chosen and is using the Christ-centered African American woman in this hour. Like Deborah she will be respected and admired for her self-denying, humble and obedient nature that can really be seen in the" Bride" of Christ.

*B. Ruth - means "friendly"*

Ruth, the great-grandmother of King David is a story of a woman with a lovely heart. She was a Moabite who married a man from Israel. After her husband, father-in-law and brother- in-law died, she was only left with her mother-in-law, Naomi and sister-in-law Orpah. Ruth and Orpah were traveling with Naomi back to her home in Israel. When they reached a certain distance, Naomi stopped to tell her two daughter-in-laws about the conditions that would confront in her homeland. She encouraged them to go back home to their own mother's house. Naomi presented them with a gloomy picture, but both girls consented to go with her.

To follow Naomi meant that both women had to walk by faith, endure more hardship and totally be rid of their old life. Therefore, the hearts of both women were exposed. But, when put to the test, what came forth from the heart of Orpah was different from Ruth. Orpah means "neck". Perhaps the reason Orpah's name means "neck," is because she possessed a "stiff neck" heart. Ruth 1:14 said, "Then they wept aloud again; and Orpah kissed her mother in-law {good-bye}, but Ruth clung to her" (Amplified Bible). The test and trails that confront us in life often help to reveal our true hearts. Once Orpah reached the borders, she was faced with two choices. She can choose to go home to her own people where she stood a better chance of being accepted and remarried, or she can choose to go with Naomi where she could possible face loneliness, rejection, and poverty. After examining her heart, we see that she was unable to resist returning back to her people.

Like Orpah, some African American women are drawn by the songs and emotionalism of Christianity. But, when it comes to commitment, they too will resist and return to the world of sin. In contrast to Orpah, what comes forth from Ruth's heart when put to the test is quite different. Ruth said, "Urge me not to leave you or to turn back from following you; for where you go I will go, and where you lodge I will lodge, your people will be my people and your God my God. Where you die I will die, and there will I be buried. The Lord do so to me and more also, if anything but death parts me from you". Ruth was willing to face her losses, put them behind her, assess her situation and cling to what little she had left. She willingly walked by faith and not by sight. Naomi talked about her God of Israel and Ruth believed in Him. When she was tried and tested, she found out how strong her faith really was. She was willing to give her life to God and do whatever was necessary to keep what little family she had left. Little did Ruth know that her faithfulness would place her in the secret place of the Most High and the road she took led her straight to overwhelming blessings. She was a caring, supportive, obedient, self-denying and humble person.

When the African American woman finds herself at a crossroad as Ruth and Orpah did, will she choose the narrow path that leads to life or the wide path that leads to destruction? Like Ruth, the African American women must be willing to face her losses, put them behind her, assess her situation and cling to what she has left. She must walk by faith and not by sight.

*C. Esther - means "star"*

Israel got into sin and fell but when they returned to God, He delivered them. Esther, a Jewess, became Queen of Persia and was sent by God to deliver Israel. King Xerxes decided to show off his wealth and power. He got drunk and called for his beautiful wife Vashti to expose her beauty to his guests. When she refused, she was dethroned. Then, God chose Esther to be queen. Before being presented to the king, Esther went through twelve months of beauty treatment. Esther was very obedient and as a result found favor with all who came in contact with her. Mordecai told her not to reveal her identity and she simply obeyed his authority. From this we can see that she was very obedient and humble. God's word says that the humble are raised up and the prideful are brought down.

The Bible described Esther as beautiful (Est.2:7). There were many other beautiful women to choose from, but what made Esther more desirable than the rest of the virgins in the eyes of the King? Vashti his first wife was beautiful and so were all the other virgins, but Esther was called and chosen by the Almighty God. Vashti might have appeared to be haughty, self-centered, controlling, dominating, rebellious, disrespectful, materialistic, conceited, selfish and prideful. She did not seem to understand her role as a Queen and his role as a king. As a result she rebelled and even embarrassed him in front of his guests.

Today we can see that African American men are faced with many challenges. If the African American woman takes the attitude of Vashti shaming her man and showing no mercy in the moment of his weakness, she will lose not only him but God's purpose for her life. However if she chooses to be merciful, humble and obedient to God, like Esther, and demonstrate the love of Jesus, this will draw him closer to the light of Jesus. They will be overwhelmingly blessed.

In contrast to the Vashti, King Xerxes had before; he was surely overtaken by more than Esther's outer beauty. He was overwhelmed by the inner beauty of Esther's gentle, loving and humble soul. She was a woman of prayer and fasting. She was also tactful, mentally perceptive, courageous, patriotic, obedient, humble and self-denying. If it were not for her obedience, self-denying love and humble spirit, Jerusalem might never have been rebuilt.

Many other great women of the Bible contributed victoriously to the making of their nation.

Women like Anna, Hannah, Mary Magdalene, Abigail and others had the same common thread abiding in their hearts. All seem to exude the spirit humbleness, self-denying love and obedience to the Almighty God. African American women must rise above the Vashti's and Orpah's of this world, and shine with the self-denying spirit of Esther. Like Deborah, they must be busy about the Father's business. Like Ruth, they must be fixed, unbending and determined to do the will of the Lord Jesus Christ like. These great women of yesterday knew the value of having a covenant with God, and the value of having a self-denying, gentle and humble *spirit.*

Today their are more and more African American women like Deborah, Ruth, Esther, Anna, Hannah, Mary Magdalene, and Abigail of the Bible who have joined forces to destroy the works of the devil. They are helping to deliver their people and others out of the vicious cycle of sin and damnation. They respect each others' ministries and support each other to fulfill God's plan and purpose.

We must strive to put on Christ's nature and be Christ-centered women. Begin to daily operate in the fruits of the Spirit - joy, patience, wisdom, meekness, knowledge, understanding, goodness, unselfishness and love. Never take cruel advantage of anyone or be quick to take offense. Do not keep a record of wrongs done to you. Practice politeness, honor, righteousness, self-control, purity and honesty. Hate sin but love the one who has sinned. The greater the agape love, the brighter you will shine. The greater the agape love, the greater the degree of fellowship with the Father, Son and Holy Spirit. Walking in agape love causes you to walk in holiness and forgiveness.

All Christ-centered women must strive to grow and remain in this kind of love and holiness until they reach Heaven. This kind of love will cause you to study to show yourself approved, pray and intercede for others, and apply the Word of God on a consistent basis. They will know you by your agape love.

Many African American women from all over the world, rich and poor, old and young are sick of sin and turning to the true and living God. They are becoming holy and upright before God. By modeling holiness, kindness and courage, they will teach the younger generation to do the same thing. The only way to live and fulfill God's purpose for your life, as a Christ-centered woman, is to totally separate yourself from the old world. God's purpose for the Christ-centered African American woman is to become a blueprint of His love, to be transformed into a holy, loving and mature witness as the Bride of Christ. Walking in love and operating by faith is the only way we can overcome the wickedness of this world in which we live.

We can compare the Christ-centered African American woman to a diamond. A diamond is extremely rare and very precious. The pure, natural carbon and other ingredients of this most important mineral resource give the stone its hardness (strength). The African American woman survived the hazardous journey from the wicked depths of slavery and she is still coming forth as pure and holy jewels. At one time the diamond was a relatively insignificant stone. Once the value of its remarkable properties became known, it became a symbol of wealth, status, power, and substance.

Just like the diamond, the Christ-centered African American woman will be valued. She will be a witness to all and through her holy and upright examples many will come out from the depths of a wicked and perverted generation. Holiness and chastity bring beauty and honor into the lives of the Christ-centered African American woman.

She is the Bride of Christ, the wise virgin and will, like a diamond, rise up and be blessed. The way to cut a diamond is with another diamond and the way to live a life of love, peace, joy and prosperity is to be transformed into the image of Christ Jesus and walk in His Kind of Love! Whatever God has for her to do, she must do it now. Woman! Now Is The Time.

## Chapter Eight

# GOD'S PLAN
# AND PURPOSE

One bright morning in January 1990, while I was in worship, God spoke to me. The congregation began to sing the song, "Lord Prepare Me to Be a Sanctuary." As we sang, God said, "Don't you sing this song to me this way anymore: you are not only in preparation, you are also maturing in my likeness. In this hour I am calling you to 'BE' my sanctuary. Now you can sing this song to me:"

*Lord, I am Your Sanctuary*

*I'm pure and holy*

*I've been tried and found true*

*And with thanksgiving*

*I am your living Sanctuary*

*Exalting You.*

There comes a time when we must grow up in the things of God. He is calling all that are His to be like Him in this hour. God's plan and purpose for you, Christ-centered woman, is to walk in His kind of love and in His forgiveness on a daily basis. God's kind of love is *agape* love. *Agape* love demonstrated within you will scatter blessings among others near and far. *Agape* love gives value to everything. It is active and self-sacrificing. It is weakest when we are young in the faith, and it grows in power with exercise and age. As we constantly grow in love, we will blossom like a beautiful flower.

*Agape* love is a power that is first placed in your heart by accepting Jesus as Lord and Savior over your life. First you will see a stem, then leaves and last, fruits. There is nothing *agape* love cannot do. It never grows weary. Nothing in the soul is superior to it. And all other feelings open to it as flowers to the sun.

*Agape* love is a measure of true manhood or womanhood. True manhood or womanhood resides in the neighborhood of *agape* love. Without *agape* love, your whole experience on this earth is worthless and inefficient. It profits nothing and gives no real honor to God. Yet, it is very important thing to God. We love Him because He first loved us. The fruit of the Spirit is *agape* love. It lies at the very foundation of Christ's character. We are rooted and grounded in love. It is the fullness and completeness of our Christian character. We are made mature in *agape* love. *Agape* love fulfills the law. If you want to enter Heaven, you must learn to walk in *AGAPE* LOVE.

You may master many languages, interpret all secret things, comprehend knowledge, be inspired by faith that moves mountains, and bestow all your goods on the poor, but without agape love it will profit you nothing. It would all be worthless in God's sight. You may have high intellect or even be genius, and you might have won high praise in this world. Regardless of your situation, good or bad, if you have not loved, all is worthless in the eyes of God.

God's requirement for all mankind to enter Heaven is to accept Christ as Lord and Savior over their lives. We must turn from all association with evil and walk in the power of forgiveness, love and faith. Realize that you must concentrate on walking daily in agape love, for *gape* love is God personified. This kind of love is very different from natural love, or what the world calls love. It makes you better, holier, and happier. *Agape* love causes you to love your family, heritage, country and mankind everywhere. Surely, as stars reflect the light of the sun, so will your spirit and soul reflect the *agape* love of God in your everyday life!

We must put on kindness and holiness. Envy and strife will lead to unfairness and cruelty. Jealousy gives the eyes a downcast look. But with *agape* love, boasting, self-pity and puffed-up pride will cease.

It is a privilege to be born again and in the kingdom of the living God. It is like being in school all over again and the world as your classroom. There is only one subject being studied, and that is *agape* love. Matthews says, "And He replied to him, you shall love the Lord your God with all your heart and with all your soul and with all your mind (intellect). This is the great (most important, principal) and first commandment. And a second is like it: You shall love your neighbor as [you do] yourself. These two commandments sum up and upon them depend all the Law and the Prophets (Matthew 22:37-40), [Amplified]." To enter into the new life as a Christian

**84**

one must be justified, in right standing with God, and most important believe in (call on) the name of Jesus (Romans 10:9-10). Jesus is your foundation. Once you receive Him, you are ready to build your new house. You now have the right to build a righteous and holy life-style within. Always keep in mind that the prerequisite is Jesus. The main subject to master is *agape* love.

While in school you must learn to apply *agape* love into your daily life. The world is where you acquire experience which fosters growth. The Bible is your textbook. Jesus is your master and the Holy Spirit is your teacher. Together they guide you and lead you to the Almighty God. What is the reward? The reward is abundant life. Become the bride of Christ and spend eternity with the Father, Son and Holy Spirit.

The privilege of living in this kingdom means you will be expected to manifest the fruit of the Spirit. Godly wisdom, knowledge, understanding, good behavior, and unselfishness must forever be demonstrated within the life of the bride of Christ. We are to owe no one but to love. Christians do not take cruel advantage of one another nor take quick offense at misdoings. They must not keep a record of evil done or said about them. They must also learn not to dominate, manipulate or control others. Neither should they allow others to control them. Christians must polite, honest, righteous, holy, chaste, kind, modest, pure, and full of joy and calm delight.

They should hate the sin but not the sinner. The greater the *agape* love, the brighter they will shine in fellowship with the Father, Son, and Holy Spirit.

The plan of God for you and for all those who want to reach Heaven is to repent, turn from evil, be born again, be holy and chaste, live in the newness of Christ and manifest *agape* love as they grow to perfection! Jesus desires us to be perfect because He is perfect. It is vital that you work on your own salvation with fear and trembling. Enter at the strait and narrow gate. God wants you to develop an inter-personal relationship with Him, His Son and with other Christ-centered men and women. God wants to love through you. *Woman! Now Is The Time.* He has a plan and a purpose for your life. Now is the time to work out the plan and have faith in God. He is the truth, the way and the life. Reach out to Him and present your body as a living sacrifice, holy and ac-ceptable in His sight.

Black woman! Remember! Jesus loves you. It does not matter where you've been, what your have done, the color of your skin, or the trials you still go through, let Him be Lord and Savior over your spirit, body and soul. God wants you to spend eternity with Him. He requires you to reflect His Nature. Woman of God, God has not forgotten you!

He is the truth, the way and the life. Reach out to Him now. Present your body as a living sacrifice, holy and acceptable in His sight.

## Chapter Nine

# NOW IS THE TIME

*M*any women have acknowledged that they are loosed from the bondage of sin but do not know how to walk in what they have been loosed into. Now is the time to walk in what you know to be truth. God Almighty has heard your humble repented cry and has laid down a spiritual foundation for you, which is Jesus Christ, the hope of glory. If you will open up your heart and by faith follow His commands and laws for your life, you will be blessed and not ashamed. You are a chosen generation, a holy nation, chosen to live holy and prosperous in your spirit, soul, and, body. He made a way for you to get out of darkness (the devil's hands) and move into His own marvelous light.

Now is the time to be strong and of good courage. Do not be afraid, or dismayed, for the Lord your God will be with you everywhere you go. God's promises are released to those who walk in covenant with Him and His Son Jesus Christ. Now is the time to surrender totally to His will and glorify Him with your life. You have been chosen to be a servant of God. He wants to transform you into a Christ-like being, changing your attitude, your walk, your talk, and every aspect of your new life.

Now is the time for you to walk in God's love, peace, joy and compassion. He has called you to be the head and not the tail, to live above all circumstances and not beneath. No longer will you defend yourself when people rebel against you openly and directly; take no offense and God will fight for you. Almighty God knows those who are His; He knows who is at fault and who is holy. He is the Judge of all things. Trust in Him and lean not unto your own understanding. Acknowledge Him in everything you do and He will send blessings upon you. Strive always to exhort your brothers and sisters with words to restore them.

You cannot and will not rest or have much peace until you walk in your purpose. He made a way for you to get out of the devil's strongholds and now He wants to move you into a place of prosperity in all areas of your new life in Christ Jesus. Now is the time to surrender totally to His Will and glorify Him with your life. Let Almighty God transform you into His likeness. He wants to humble you as He changes your attitude, walk, and talk. God has a plan and purpose for your life. Listen to what God is saying to you in the following poem:

NOW IS THE TIME!

Now is the time to let your light shine

In and around you like never before.

To let go of the bonds

And let My love abound.

That is My plan for you in this land.

**89**

Listen closely to the Word

And let the Holy Spirit take control.

My plan for you will begin to grow;

And destroy the course that the evil one

Put in place for you and your loved ones.

NOW IS THE TIME TO BE SET FREE!

I know your pain is very deep within

And the scars can still be seen beneath,

But if you listen to Me

You will be healed

In word and in deed!

For I am the answer and I have the key

That will deliver and set you free!

Let Me in and you will see

The blessings that I have for you.

Your harsh voice and unkind words

Will surely cease.

You will gently address your children

With kindness and ease.

Your word will change

From bitter to sweet, sweet, sweet.

Erasing all the old stains and pain

That was put there when sin entered in.

And let your heart be filled

With praise, praise, praise.

I will inhabit you

And your enemies will flee.

No evil will befall you,

Nor will any plague come near.

I am all-powerful and I have no fear.

NOW IS THE TIME TO LET

MY KIND OF LOVE OVERFLOW!

I have promised you many years of life

On earth but even that is not long enough

For you to walk completely in line.

There is no time to be stubborn!

No need to hide your face from Me.

Just let your heart, believe and receive,

And you will be free, free, free

Your final chance is at hand.

If you choose to follow My commands,

You will have victory in this land.

NOW IS THE TIME TO BE MY DELIGHT

So change your heart and get a brand new start!

Let mercy and grace abound and walk

Day by day in the spirit of forgiveness.

No longer can your heart be filled with

Bitterness, pain, foul words, and unforgiveness

From sin deep within.

Love, joy, peace and prosperity come

From within and will overflow.

If you walk in what you know.

NOW IS THE TIME TO GET IN LINE

AND BE VICTORIOUS IN ME!

Take the selfishness out of your heart.

Give the Holy Spirit room to move

Peace will be yours forever, and the bondage,

I tell you, will be broken over you,

Oh, take heed, My child,

Admit your defeat and turn to Me,

Let My glory fill your spirit,

Place my loving words deep within.

And let your eyes stay fixed on Me.

All your hopes and dreams will be fulfilled.

If you obey, believe, and receive!

I have chosen you to be My example

For all the world to see!

It must begin with you

And continue till the end of time!


NOW IS THE TIME TO WALK IN ONENESS
WITH ME!


## THREE CRUCIAL POINTS

Let's look at three crucial points that the poems bring out that are necessary for the African American woman to consider if she is to live as an overcomer.

1) Look eye to eye at your life.

2) Decide the direction you will take.

3) Get the plan for which you were created.

## STEP ONE

## LOOK EYE TO EYE AT YOUR LIFE

Let a man examine himself

1Corinthians 11:28

A young girl expressed her hatred of this world. "People are so cruel and so mean," she yelled in a fury. Yet, when you step back and look at her actions, you will find that she is just as cruel and selfish as the persons that she is describing. She hated being an African American woman. She tried to hide herself in sexual relationships that never lasted more than for a few months. Her most serious relationship was with a married man. She became extremely hostile and was involved in fights. Then she got pregnant and ended up on welfare.

So many of our young women crave for love and affection but are looking in all the wrong places. They don't realize that they receive what they give out. It is in giving that we receive. This is why it is more blessed to give than to take what is given. Many women have accepted the evil that was said about them and now their children are giving out the evil and reaping a bad harvest from their wrong motives for giving. We must strive to put an end to this vicious cycle of sin and destruction that plague our households.

As a first step, take a look into your own heart and get to know the real self. Secondly, examine the company you are entertaining. Birds of a feather flock together (Ps.1; Prov. 13:20). Next, examine your habits (1Jn 2:15). Finally, examine your thoughts, affections and motives (Ps.10:4; Prov. 23:7). The Scripture warns us that, "As a man thinketh in his heart so is he," and "To be carnally minded is death" (Rom.8:6; Col.3:17; 1Cor.10:31). Are you striving to please self or God?

Now get in front of a large mirror. Look at yourself and ask these questions. What are my motives for helping others? What kind of feelings, words and thoughts spring forth out of my heart? Do I say what I mean and mean what I say? Do I do things so that I can be accepted? Do I try to take matters into my own hands? Am I so self-sufficient I do not need or want anyone else to help me? Do I control others or let others control my life? Am I so timid that I let others continue to use and abuse me? Am I filled with anger or fear most of the time? Do I criticize others and try to tell them how to run their business?

Do I meddle into other people's affairs? Do I like certain kinds of people and ignore and dislike others? Do I talk ill of others? Am I jealous? Am I selfish? Do I laugh and poke fun at others? Do I talk down to adult of children? Do I hate being African American and wish I were another color? Do I have hate in my heart when I see a brother with a woman of another race? Do I gossip and feed myself with soap operas, pornography, elicit relationships, drugs, cigarettes, gluttony or alcohol?

If you can say yes to any of the above it is time to move to step number two.


STEP TWO

## DECIDE THE DIRECTION YOU WILL TAKE

LIFE / AN OPEN DOOR

REV. 3:8

What is the meaning of life? The life that is in Christ Jesus is a place of:

a. Safety - protection, defense, strength, security.

b. Plenty -wealth, abundance, riches, prosperity, success, well- being, property, substance, victory.

c. Fellowship (unity, oneness, wholeness, peace, compatibility, goodwill, companionship, friendship.

The way to life is an open door. Jesus Christ has made this door open to us by His death, burial, and resurrection. He was obedient unto death. Now you can enter into a new way of living, reserved only for the Bride of Christ.

The gate is so narrow that each person must strip off sin in order to enter. Self-righteousness, carnality, cursing, controlling others, thinking evil thoughts, deceitfulness, wickedness of heart and worldliness must be stripped off. You must strive to seek to enter the strait gate at all cost. What does it profit a man to gain the whole world and lose his soul? The word of God says "For the wages of sin is death." (Romans 6:23) It is easier going downhill than it is uphill. There is only one possible way to destruction and the way is fatal. That is a guarantee. You must count the cost. The cost of sin is eternal damnation.

STEP THREE

## GET THE PLAN FOR WHICH YOU

## WERE CREATED

A SEARCH FOR HIS BRIDE

GENESIS 24

In Genesis 24:4 Abraham, out of the love for his son Issac, sought to find him a wife. He eagerly planned ahead to prepare a blessing for his beloved son. Just like In like fashion, God the Father saw

**97**

that it is was good for His Son Jesus to have a bride. This is a beautiful picture of Christ and the Church (Eph.5:32). The church was chosen before the foundation of the world to be the Bride of Christ. Issac had received his father's inheritance and the fullness of his blessings. Abraham sent this servant Eliezer on a mission to find a bride for his son (Gen. 24:2). This was Rebecca who represents the Church/ the Bride of Christ. Like Jesus, Eliezer did not speak of himself (Gen. 24:33) Abraham, like the Father, revealed the plans to his son (John 14:53; John 16:14). Eliezer would not eat bread until he had completed his errand. (Gen. 24:33) The Holy Spirit cannot fellowship with us until He has revealed to us the character of the Father and Son.

Rebekah represents a type of the Church - called out by the Spirit of God and separated unto the Name of Jesus. "Wilt thou go with this man?" Rebekah said, "I will go" Gen 24.58. The call of the Holy Spirit is personal "Wilt thou go?" And it is urgent "Hinder Me not" (Gen.24:33, 56). Rebekah counted the cost and left all behind and followed the man. Along the way to Abraham's house, she had not seen him, but loved and rejoiced in the hope of meeting him face to face. In the meantime, Eliezer taught her about Abraham and Issac and groomed her for meeting him. This is how it is with the Holy Spirit. He will teach you all truth. He will lead, instruct and guide you in the way that you should go. He prepares you for the Groom.

If we follow the Holy Spirit and do not grieve Him, we will experience love, peace and joy forever. You are here to learn to be the Bride of Christ. You must be presented holy and undefiled. Let the Holy Spirit transform you into the likeness of Christ. You have been called out and must make a decision to leave your old ways of doing things to enter into a new and victorious life, which is entered into by faith. Faith puts God in charge.

Mother, daughter, sister, and friend if there has ever been a time for you to shine, NOW IS THE TIME! If there has ever been a time for you to demonstrate agape love, NOW IS THE TIME. First you must be born again, filled with the Holy Spirit, be willing to be transformed through the power of faith, love and forgiveness, and stand firm on the Word of God. Be determined in your heart to be that beacon of light for the Lord. Look eye to eye at your life situation. Receive and accept the truth that the Lord creates wealth overflowing for you also. Now you can begin to reap the special harvest prepared by the Father and the Son just for you, the Bride. You will find peace in the mist of a storm and inexpressible joy and calm delight when you walk in your destiny. WOMAN! NOW IS THE TIME.

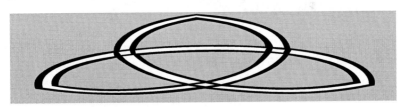

# APPENDIX

## GOD'S LOVE LIFTED ME

I was sinking deep within
Far from the peace of God.
Oppression had me bound within
Thinking I'd never rise again.

Then the Father heard my cry
He told me to get rid of pride.
Selfishness, you must deny
Now put My love inside.

So I threw away my pride
and received God's love inside
God's love lifted me
Love set me free.

Superwoman I was called
Thou being abused and misused,
Overworked, tired, and confused.
I didn't know what to say or do

Then the Lord appeared to me
With so much love and open arms
Turn from the world and turn to me
And I will set you free.
Now I am free, I am free indeed
Free from the world of sin

Depriving myself of selfish things
Striving to please My King.

*Agape* love I have received and
It takes care of my every need
The Holy Spirit guides my way
From day to day and I will not stray.

Yes, love lifted me,
When I threw away my pride
Yes, Jesus made me whole
When I turned from the world of sin
Now love, joy and peace are released
Deep down within my soul.
I turned from the world to Jesus
And I was totally set free
Jesus is all I need and
He takes care of my every need.

# Order Form
### Postal Address

INSTITUTE OF HIGHER LIVING PUBLISHERS
P.O. Box 888731
Atlanta, GA 30356

ISBN 0-9647046-9-2

Please send: ***God Has Not Forgotten You! Now is the Time***
to:

Name: _____

Address: _____

City: _____

Telephone (_____) _____

E-mail _____

**Book Price:**   $14.95 in U.S. dollars
**Shipping:**   $3.00 for the first book, and $1.00 for each additional book to cover shipping and handling within U.S, Canada, and Mexico. International orders, add $6.00 for the first book and $3.00 for each additional book.